THE
BLUFFER'S
GUIDE TO
PSYCHOLOGY

WARREN MANSELL

Oval Books

Published by Oval Books
335 Kennington Road
London SE11 4QE
United Kingdom

Telephone: +44 (0)20 7582 7123
Fax: +44 (0)20 7582 1022
E-mail: info@ovalbooks.com
Web site: www.ovalbooks.com

First printed 2005

Series Editor – Anne Tauté

Cover designer – Vicki Towers
Cover image – © Corbis
Printer – Gopsons Papers Ltd.
Producer – Oval Projects Ltd.

The Bluffer's® Guides series is based
on an original idea by Peter Wolfe.

The Bluffer's Guide®, The Bluffer's Guides®,
Bluffer's®, and Bluff Your Way® are
Registered Trademarks.

ISBN-13: 978-1-903096-63-5
ISBN-10: 1-903096-63-4

CONTENTS

WHAT IS PSYCHOLOGY?

Psychology literally means the study of the mind (from the Greek 'psyche' meaning 'mind' and 'logos' meaning 'study'). While it is impressive to know Ancient Greek in itself, you will need a few more clues to master the subject. Firstly, it is essential to grasp the fundamental facts because so few others do. This will put you head and shoulders above the rest – even most psychologists. The fact that at the heart of psychology of any kind lie insoluble problems is an absolute boon to bluffers. Even its terminology is full of contradictions. Make the most of it at all times.

Secondly, psychology means different things to different people. So, to bluff in this field you will need to know your source material – psychology and the many 'schools' it has spawned. The different schools within psychology have a level of mutual tolerance rivalling that of most fundamentalist religions. There are the Experimental Psychologists and the Applied Psychologists, the former laboratory bound, the latter rootling around in the real world. There are the Psychoanalysts, who believe that psychology is largely about studying the unconscious irrational forces that affect people; and the Behaviourists, who believe that psychology is about studying the causes and effects of behaviour. There are even sects such as Cognitive-Behavioural Analysts, a minority rarely encountered, who actually listen to other groups of psychologists. Feel free to adopt one of the existing definitions of psychology, or like everyone else, make up your own.

Before we equip you with the essential facts, findings and, most importantly, the particular 'persona' of a psychologist, here are some reassuring points to relax you into the role. They will foster your appreciation that bluffing in this field is not only easy and effortless, but may often be essential.

1. **Not even psychologists themselves are sure exactly what psychology is**. Psychologists are obsessed with pointing out that the definition of any concept within psychology, such as intelligence, memory or emotion, is not precise. This also applies to psychology itself.

2. **To be a psychologist it is not strictly necessary to practise psychology**. It is a frustrating fact for many psychologists that some of the most influential theories in psychology were developed by philosophers, psychiatrists and other medics, biologists, computer scientists, physicists, engineers and Great Uncle Walter. Fortunately, the theories of the human mind developed by traffic wardens have never really caught on.

3. **Few people know what a psychologist does**. There are so many disciplines of psychology that it is impossible to pin down what the day-to-day behaviour of a psychologist might involve, so a lay person will often accept any answer, e.g., "talking to people", "reading people's minds", "extracting memories of radio jingles from people's brains and weighing them".

4. **Every psychologist has his or her own theory**. Don't feel obliged to be well versed in other people's ideas when you can be well versed in your own. The range is virtually limitless, from confirming what people think might be true (only using real experiments, e.g., "Is the grass really greener on the other side?"), through investigating something that everyone else has casually overlooked (e.g., "The study of a new basic emotion: smuglausitude"), to simply exploring the role of psychology in one facet of human behaviour (e.g. "The function of selective attention in scanning for a free barman in a crowded pub").

5. **Great expectations**. If there is one underlying principle behind all psychology (which there probably isn't), it is that people's expectations dictate their behaviour, whether these expectations come from their unconscious drives, their learned experiences, their social role, or their current perceptions. The way out of this apparent mental straitjacket is to learn to expect the unexpected and to learn not always to expect the expected. Or, put more simply, you can sum up over a century of research in psychology with the phrase, "Smile! It may never happen." Of course you must never express this mundane view in a room full of psychologists. Instead you need to share the illusion that the complex terms and convoluted explanations that populate the discipline are absolutely necessary.

Now you know what psychology really is, you have a secure base from which to explore the finer points of the discipline, and to begin to comprehend this curious identity. The first step is a big one, but nonetheless straightforward to master. Psychology – science, art or humanity? To a psychologist there is only one real answer to this question.

WHY PSYCHOLOGY REALLY IS A SCIENCE

'Hard' scientists (such as those researching physics and the biochemistry of the nematode worm) often question the status of psychology as a science. Most sensible people, who have managed to escape science as a profession, regard psychology as common sense dressed up in obscure terminology ('psychobabble').

However, should you wish to impress a psychologist, you must cling tenaciously to the view that psychology really is a science. To appreciate this claim you need to know some History. This is, of course, a humanity, but don't let that put you off because you need not know any more about the history of psychology than a psychologist, which is very little.

The Early Days:
Philosophy gets quizzed for evidence

The history of psychology is really quite brief. For over 2,500 years everyone was happy to let philosophers do all the psychology (good examples are Aristotle, Socrates, and, after a while, Descartes – who can be blamed for splitting the mind away from the body as 'the ghost in the machine'). These mental meanderers speculated about the human mind without any scientists bothering them with a little thing called 'evidence'. Eventually, at the end of the 19th century, they were rumbled. Scientists wanted to see some proof that the philosophers' outlandish claims had any grain of truth – and so the era of Empirical Psychology was born.

From this point on, big ideas about the mind began to be subjected to the **Experimental Method** – i.e., by proposing a theory, and then testing whether what you predicted would happen does in fact happen. If it doesn't, then that's one nail in the coffin of the theory. Or so it goes.

Unfortunately, psychologists are only human and therefore prone to being impressionable or stubborn in equal measure, so some theories go out of fashion despite being supported, and others persist doggedly without a shred of evidence.

You may wish to know that the first psychology laboratory was founded in 1879 at the University of Leipzig by **Wilhelm Wundt** (1832-1920), but only if you plan to talk to a German. Wundt began a long line of **Gestalt*** Psychologists in Germany, who were early experts in visual perception – the study of how people experience and categorise what is placed before their eyes (and ears, nose, and so forth). Their well-known conclusion was 'the whole is greater than the sum of its parts', a principle that not only applies to optical illusions but also to matchstick cathedrals, fairy cakes and Abba.

William James (1842-1910), brother of the novelist Henry James, was the flamboyant American rival of Wundt. He helpfully defined psychology as 'the science of mental life' and slaved for 12 years to produce his landmark book, *The Principles of Psychology* (which you will make a point of referring to as 'The James'). James famously formulated the James-Lange Theory of Emotions in 1884, a year before Carl Lange (1834-1900) stumbled upon the same idea.

The James-Lange theory states that an awareness of emotion occurs as a consequence of one's physical reactions to an experience. James illustrated this with an example endlessly quoted by psychologists which is that you become aware of feeling afraid of a charging bear only after you have already reacted to it (for example by running away, or by making a mental note to avoid a holiday in Yosemite National Park next year).

It is worth knowing that psychologists are still wrangling with the complexities of the James-Lange theory today, which either goes to show how difficult psychology is (it really is a 'hard' science) or how hopeless most psychologists are at doing proper science.

* German for pattern. Pronounce 'Geshtalt' for maximum effect.

The In-Between Years:
Psychology loses sight of evidence

While the empirical psychologists were wrestling with making psychology a bona fide science, **Sigmund Freud** (1856-1939), who was actually a psychiatrist, came along with his new field of Psychoanalysis and spoiled it. Freud was not inclined to subject his ideas to scientific tests and so they are no longer quite at home in a psychology textbook which, if you've ever read a psychology textbook, is a great recommendation for them.

Despite this, Freud was the first to fully explain the role of parents' relationships with their children and their impact on the conflicts within the unconscious mind during adulthood. In a significant way, Freud was the 'father' of psychology: he has nurtured a deep unconscious (and conscious) conflict between psychologists right up to the present day. We recommend you read to Freud's stimulating ideas in private, but remember to maintain your credentials by berating him in public for his lack of scientific rigour. Speaking ill of the dead seems to be permitted as far as Freud is concerned.

The Era of Behaviourism:
Psychology demands evidence again (and is very strict about it)

The rise of psychoanalysis was fought tooth-and-nail by a parallel movement reclaiming the scientific moral high-ground. This was Behaviourism, propounded by **John Watson** (1878-1958), **Ivan Pavlov** (1849-1936) and **B. F. Skinner** (1904-90). Watson did not value introspection and empathy quite as much as his psychoanalytic contemporaries. He proclaimed:

'The goal of psychology is not the understanding of experience but the prediction and control of behaviour!' To this end, behaviourists created unnatural contraptions such as the 'Skinner Box' (q.v.) to observe and manipulate the responses of rats, dogs and pigeons which purported to inform them about the day-to-day behaviour of humans.

The behaviourists shunned the study of a person's personal experiences as if it were a dubious fashion and relegated it to somewhere between mysticism and telling fibs. Mental experience was described as an 'epiphenomenon', which means that it occurs on the surface as a consequence of real things happening but has no impact on anyone or anything. Rather like a political manifesto then.

The Cognitive Revolution:
Psychology becomes obsessed with computers (just like everyone else)

A new movement called Cybernetics emerged in the 1940s and '50s led by American mathematician **Norbert Wiener** (1894-1964) and which again gave the mind centre stage. In Cybernetics the human mind is regarded as a complicated kind of thermostat which regulates its surroundings to maintain a comfortable experience. If you claim knowledge of this movement, no-one will doubt your credentials as a specialist because it lasted only a brief time before transmuting into the gargantuan discipline known today as **Cognitive Psychology**.

Cognitive Psychologists proposed the influential idea that one can study the human mind on the basis that it works like a computer. One might assume a major stumbling block to this idea is the fact that

11

psychologists know even less about how a computer works. They had just managed to create an analogy that the mind is the 'software' running on the 'hardware' of the brain when genuine brain scientists reminded them that this analogy was also pointless. Computers are designed to be virtually identical whereas no two brains are alike except, perhaps, in the case of Tony Blair and Dubya Bush.

The End Result:
Confusion

As you can see, Psychology seems to progress using colourful analogies. Over the period of a hundred years, the science of human behaviour has been based on that of a dog, a rat, a pigeon, a thermostat, a computer and, no doubt soon, a fruit machine. Only the philosophers can be credited with the original (and somehow more sensible) idea that the study of the human mind should be based on the mind of a human.

The net effect of the many movements within psychology is that there is little time to learn about all of them and each psychologist clings to his or her own precious discipline, while insisting that the others are as relevant as a Tree-Hugging Collective.

So, while psychologists in general may claim to understand the minds of other people, one psychologist will rarely understand what another psychologist is talking about. Happily this leaves you free to select your preferred field and take a lofty stance with the others. For example, say:

– to a behaviourist: "If my thoughts are an epiphenomenon, then I assume you won't be upset by my thinking that your tie is inexcusably loud."

12

- to a cognitive psychologist: "If a computer is like the human mind, then tell me what it is that my laptop really wants in life."
- to a psychoanalyst after he or she has inferred your deep unconscious motives from the way you are holding your tea-cup: "Fascinating. How do you think my teabag is feeling?"

HOW TO ACT LIKE A PSYCHOLOGIST

Bluffing knowledge of psychology is pretty straight-forward. However, it barely qualifies someone as a psychologist. So we are going to leave these details until later. In practice, psychology is less about pluck-ing droplets of insight from a fountain of knowledge and more like shoving your fingers into a leaky dam to stem the deluge of ignorance. The skill is to make the latter seem like the former.

Develop an Air

First is one's manner. Psychologists manage to foster an unnerving air of aloofness, self-sacrifice and absent-mindedness which, in combination, will thor-oughly perplex their opposition. The general attitude is of the kind: "I forgot your birthday because I have been very busy thinking of clever ways of how I might advance science and/or help people."

The budding psychologist needs a semblance of social skills, but will focus them solely on turning the topic of conversation round to his own limited area of expertise. When he has his victim in sight, he launches his secret weapon – the rambling explanation. For instance, "Your cat sounds very intelligent. Tell me, how does Tiddles respond to moving objects in his peripheral vision? You don't know? Well let me explain with a little example…"

Acquire Impressive Curios

The second necessary factor to cultivate a double-life as a psychologist is props. Many a psychologist's office will contain the ubiquitous Phrenology Head – a mock ivory model of a bald sexless human from the neck up, with personality traits mapped on different areas of the skull. It was most likely bought in a peak of excitement by the psychologist's mother as a graduation present. Of course, any self-respecting psychologist realises that this model provides no genuine information and is absolutely useless. But the fact that it demonstrates the thrill of discovery of the Victorian era gives it a certain charm. Serious psychologists may often offset this by proudly placing a large detailed diagram of the brain on the wall. This carries a great deal of intricate information and, to a psychologist, is just as useless.

The icing on the cake is a well-placed cartoon that gently ridicules psychology. It helps to give visitors the impression that the psychologists do not take their work too seriously (which of course they do). In the 'real world' outside the office or laboratory, psychologists do not have recourse to the impressive props of other professions like white coats and wigs. The best protection, therefore, is to grow a beard and develop an Austrian accent which, while extreme, is as effective as wearing a bright gold badge saying "I'm a Psychologist".

Fend Off Tricky Questions

Third is how to deal with non-psychologists (or the 'normal' population as psychologists like to call them). In any ordinary social event, the average psychologist will encounter many apparently intelligent people who seem to lose all command of logic when faced with a psychologist, and endow this individual with what can only be described as special powers.

"So, can you tell what I'm thinking?" is the most common response. You can answer in two ways, essentially "No" or "Yes". "No" is the truth, not only because mind-reading is impossible, but because most psychologists are below average at reading social signals. Why else would they have to study theories of human behaviour when to other people it comes naturally? "Yes" is an outright lie, but leads to a far more interesting conversation.

When talking to 'normals', it is often just as important to know what is not true in psychology as it is to know what is an established fact. One common myth the bluffing psychologist should dismiss with an air of absolute assurance is that people only use 10% of their brains. This myth (which appeared with the rise of commercial mental improvement courses in 1930s America) is False, with the possible exception of certain psychologists.

On occasions, people other than psychologists will expect a psychologist in their midst actually to know something about the mind. Questions range from being difficult to answer, to having no answer at all, to being just silly. For example, 'How do we learn to speak?', 'What is happiness?', and 'Why is belly button fluff always blue?' Here are some helpful responses pioneered by psychologists alongside their real meanings:

Helpful Response	Real Meaning
"There are several explanations but none fully account for all the evidence."	The only psychological explanation I know sounds too much like common sense.
"It's an empirical question."	No-one has bothered to test it.
"It's a question of semantics."	I haven't a clue what you mean.
"I would be interested to know how you explain it."	My mind has gone blank for a moment.
"That's not my specific area of expertise."	Neither is 99% of psychology.

There is only one common question that can be guaranteed to make a psychologist stumble: 'So what motivated you to become a psychologist?' This is clearly an example of a crafty person trying to play a psychologist at their own game. Being a sly bluffer, you will have prepared a suitably evasive answer in advance (e.g., "At the time, it seemed slightly more meaningful than becoming an accountant"). This avoids the risk of engaging in any kind of painful self-revelation.

In private, most psychologists believe they are motivated to study psychology because it is such an exciting and stimulating area of science, but that sadly, rival psychologists are driven by strident ambition and the desperate need for power and success. They publicly lament the loss of the halcyon days when psychology could be studied with just a pen, paper, false moustache and a handful of gullible undergraduates, whereas today the science is driven by money, computer technology and brain-scanners the size of a small shed. But then there is real life, and that $10,000 research proposal on 'The role of the frontal lobes in the ability to surf the Internet'.

HOW DO NORMAL PEOPLE BECOME PSYCHOLOGISTS?

In its short history, Psychology has permeated the everyday world. A close friend may be an 'introvert' with a 'complex' who needs 'closure'. Many people believe they can pass off an understanding of psychology by watching a reality TV show and buying the latest popular self-help guide that compares each human emotion to a different garden vegetable. To rise above this populist zeitgeist, you need to be equipped with the real facts about becoming a psychologist in 21st-century society.

Stage 1. Getting the Right Qualifications at School

Psychology is now one of the most popular subjects to study at degree level. No-one seems to be aware of this stiff competition, so many potential students find themselves turned down at the first hurdle with their A-levels in English Literature, Media Studies and Basket Weaving. For the budding teenage psychologist, Biology is an absolute must, and it is safest to study at least one other 'hard' science, like Chemistry, or Physics if you are really daring. You may wish to point out that knowing Boyle's Gas Law would be considerably less useful in a psychology degree than understanding the human depths inherent in the works of Shakespeare. But this is beside the point. What is more important is to show faith that psychology is a science.

Stage 2. Getting a Degree

Getting a degree is the essential ingredient for practising psychology, but it is probably the least onerous stage once you have got on the course. While most courses are based in science departments, only the most eminent institutions, such as Oxford, Cambridge and (yes) Bristol, insist on calling their degrees Experimental Psychology. Most courses teach an exciting spattering of areas including Social Psychology, Developmental Psychology, and some of the old chestnuts such as Psychoanalysis.

The first year of the degree is spent splitting time between acting as guinea pigs for other students' experiments and learning all the psychology you could have learned at school if only the teachers hadn't dismissed it as a soft option. The final year is spent doing a research project, which most students are shocked to discover can actually lead to scientific advances in the area. This realisation tends to kick in after three weeks in their first job as a marketing assistant.

Stage 3. Choosing a Specialty

After three years spent consuming alcohol and chasing members of the opposite sex, it comes as a shock to most psychology students that they need to think seriously about their occupation. The path before them divides into two: Professional or Academic, or an uneasy combination of the two.

The Academic route begins with a PhD (which stands for Doctor of Philosophy, much to the chagrin of a psychologist). The life of an academic psychologist can be summed up in a few lines. Half one's time is spent in the student common room desperately persuading psychology undergraduates to help with the research, and the other half is spent in front of a computer desperately persuading the statistics programs to help with the research findings.

The many lives of the Professional psychologist are considerably more colourful. You can easily identify the professional routes by their 'big brother' professions: Law (Forensic Psychology), Medicine (Clinical or Health Psychology), Business (Occupational Psychology) and Teaching (Educational Psychology). There the similarity ends in that psychologists form a tiny minority of each of these professions and are usually paid much less. Given that one of the strongest drives of a psychologist is to be needed by other people, this set-up is simply ideal.

You can convey an even greater familiarity with the profession if you can casually mention one or two rarer applied areas. Just for starters there is Sports Psychology, Environmental Psychology, and Economic Psychology. One applied field as yet to be created is Motivational Gastronomic Telepsychology (the scientific analysis of supposedly humorous TV cooks).

Stage 4. Training In a Specialty

Training as a professional psychologist is not for the faint-hearted. Competition is fierce because places are tight and no-one is budging. However, the outward signs of rivalry are concealed beneath the veneer of what a psychologist would regard as 'socially appropriate human behaviour'. The skill to cultivate during training is juggling: learning the theory, putting it into practice, doing yet more research, while still maintaining a 'balanced' life. If you meet a Clinical Psychologist, congratulate him or her for getting on to a course in the first place. If you meet an Educational Psychologist, congratulate him or her for getting through the training (they have to train as a teacher too). And if you meet a Forensic Psychologist, waste no time in contacting the WWF and registering the person as an endangered species.

EXPERIMENTS IN PSYCHOLOGY

The next area to master is the 'Experiment'. When those around you twitch nervously as you mention this word, their minds full of images of innocent volunteers being zapped with electricity, you can reassuringly explain to them (with a degree of condescension, if it all possible) that these kinds of experiments have always been rare, and are certainly not practised at present. A modern-day psychology experiment is more likely to reach the threatening levels of pressing buttons on a computer or rating the attractiveness of different body odours. Despite their lack of fizzing electrodes, experiments like these are at the root of psychology.

Psychology needs experiments like Literature needs books and Medicine needs cadavers. Unfortunately you can no more guarantee a perfect experiment than you can ensure a publishable literary work or a perfect body. There are basically three kinds of research studies in psychology (but don't hold us to it), only one of which is a 'true' experiment.

Questionnaire Studies

These are rarely the most exciting forms of research. Most often they involve psychologists drafting surveys for people to complete. This process has unfortunate flaws, not least because it relies on the respondents being utterly honest and having the self-awareness of a Buddhist monk. Our advice is to ignore the blatant problems with questionnaire research. They are so fundamental to psychology that few psychologists would ever admit that the whole enterprise could be unsound. Your role as an apparent expert in this field is to quietly join this conspiracy of silence.

Most questionnaires use what is known as a **Likert Scale**. This is usually a line marked with a series of numbers on a page. The volunteer puts a cross on the line to indicate how much he or she believes each statement on the questionnaire. The psychologist of course ensures that the question is worded in plain English and is clear in meaning, e.g:

"I rarely often wish that my uncertainty was less certain."

Completely disagree 0-1-2-3-4-5-6-7-8-9-10 Completely agree

Most Likert scales go from zero to ten, but the keen participant who wants to show that extra little bit of belief may try going up to eleven.

Correlational Studies

These set out to show that people who experience or do one thing also tend to experience or do another thing. For example, one well-known study showed that children who score high on intelligence tests have more books in their homes. The problem of course is in knowing which came first. Psychologists want to know whether parents of intelligent children are more intelligent themselves and therefore buy more books, or whether books 'cause' high intelligence. The latter, you may muse, is very unlikely, especially if they are all Jeffrey Archer novels.

The 'True' Experiment

While 99% of research in psychology may be either obvious or uninformative or both, the classic 1% of experiments is both unexpected and interesting. They are like good magic tricks with the secrets revealed, and they involve a considerable amount of bluffing on the part of the psychologist.

If you have one or two classic experiments under your belt, you can masquerade as an authority. The first classic is the creation of **Stanley Milgram** in the 1960s. He tested the extent of people's obedience to a persuasive 'teacher' in a fake experiment – a worrying demonstration of the control that a psychologist can have. Those taking part were told to turn a dial to give increasingly dangerous electric shocks to a man in the next room who was screaming with pain. What they didn't know was that the whole experiment was fake. A staggering 65% of people continued until the end, when the man played dead or unconscious. The conclusion (which you should labour for its wide social ramifications) is that the power of authority can overpower one's natural empathy; or never believe what a psychologist tells you.

The second classic study also tells a salutary tale. In the early 1950s, **Solomon Asch** devised a simple study (rare in psychology). Volunteers were asked to judge which of three differently lengthed lines was the same length as another line. Nearly everyone who did this task by themselves made no errors. But, when the volunteer was asked to do it within a group of people, all of whom suggested an incorrect line, he agreed with the others. Of course, all the people in the group were accomplices of the psychologist. The conclusion (which you should make sound as profound as possible) is that one's personal perceptions of the world can be easily influenced by other people. Or maybe just that judgments of size can be a matter of opinion.

It is worth remembering during any animated discussion that whatever claim you find yourself making, there will nearly always be an experiment to back it up. If a bold opponent challenges your sources, be creative. Make the reference obscure, and therefore sound at once both scholarly and untraceable. Have it originate from, say, "the Special Issue of the *International Bi-Quarterly Journal of Subliminal Biosocial Psychometrics*" (which does not exist but your audience will be none the wiser). This ploy is the academic equivalent of claiming to have seen one of first Rolling Stones' gigs in early '61 in the back room of an East-End pub.

SOME IMPORTANT AREAS

Nothing better represents psychology than a flavour of the diverse and contradictory disciplines it has spawned. Here are some of the most prominent, and bluffable, examples with which to furnish yourself. Be wary because you will stand out like a sore thumb if you allege to know about all of them – no real psychologist has a working knowledge of more than one or two. So pick your favourite, pretend to have an intense obsession with it, and garnish this fixation with a few needless facts and figures.

Perception and Attention

'Perception' is how people experience the world. It partly depends on bottom-up processes – not double vision after a night on the town, but the information or 'stimuli' that one receives from the outside world. Perception also depends on top-down processes, which refer to people's own ideas and expectations that affect what they actually see (hear, feel, etc. – we've been here before). You only need to know one name in this area: **Richard Gregory**. He is the longstanding British cognitive psychologist who edits the *Oxford Companion of the Mind*, a weighty thousand-page tome that has become the psychology 'bible', although slightly less racy than the holy version.

You can think of the whole of Cognitive Psychology as the study of top-down processes. A commonly cited example of a top-down process in action is given by an invitation to read the following:

Paris
in the
the Spring

If you missed the two 'the's, then you were affected by a top-down process: expecting to see a grammatical sentence. If you saw both of the 'the's, then you are either a psychologist who is reading this book because you are still not sure what psychology is, in which case you are probably not alone, or you are not a psychologist but you know how crafty they can be so you studied the sentence in detail. Well done. Expert bluffing involves anticipating your subject's moves.

The earliest perceptual experts, the German Gestalt Psychologists of the late 19th century, observed that the mind has certain rules it uses to organise what it sees. For example, the illusion of two silhouetted heads facing each other that can also be interpreted as a white vase on a black background. Optical illusions were designed by psychologists to show how people's minds play tricks on them. Maybe it is more fitting to say that it is psychologists who have played tricks on people's minds by producing optical illusions in the first place. The mind would probably work quite happily without them and would not normally make the embarrassing faux-pas of identifying two people's heads as a vase.

In the 1940s, the British psychologist **Donald Broadbent** heralded the arrival of Cognitive Psychology with his work on selective attention. He described it as a 'mental filter', claiming that from the wealth of things going on all around them, people only focus on the important things, like today's football results or whether Julia Roberts is going to risk another wave at the crowd. Psychologists have called this issue the 'cocktail party problem': how you filter out a tedious conversation about mortgage rates when you are trying to eavesdrop on a nearby conversation about the surprising uses of a sink plunger.

To show that you can master the cocktail party problem you probably need to know the essence of a long, convoluted debate which is still unresolved: whether the selection of what is important is early or late, i.e., early and based on physical features (like a person's appearance) or late and based on meaning (such as what a person says). Whenever you are faced with this kind of two-way debate (and there are many in psychology), the answer is to go down the middle. "Surely it depends on the context?" is a classic parry that will always impress a psychologist.

As you may be becoming aware, psychologists love finding out things about the mind that are counter-intuitive, maybe in a vain attempt to distract everyone from the more obvious, common-sense results. To this end, the field of Perception and Attention is perfect. The following examples would mark you out as an expert in this dark art (sorry, science):

1. The Change (or Inattentional) Blindness Effect

This is a classic set of studies that gives a hint that some psychologists do not always take their work completely seriously. Researchers at Harvard showed a group of volunteers a video of a basketball match and instructed them to follow the path of the ball between players. During the match a woman dressed in a gorilla suit walked through the game and stopped to beat her chest to the camera. Amazingly, only half of the volunteers noticed the gorilla. According to the authors of this and similar studies, it shows that people only hold a very small fraction of what they see in their minds (normally the figure at the front of the scene) while neglecting the rest of it. However, you might contest that an experiment substituting the gorilla for a herd of giraffes in pink aprons would have blown this theory.

2. The Cross-Modal Perception Effect

Here, volunteers in experiments can be made (literally) to feel things using their hearing, or hear things using their sight. Lip-reading is one example. If people are played one sound (e.g., 'tah') and shown a mouth uttering a different sound (e.g., 'dah'), they report hearing the sound they see. This effect is even stronger in those with a condition called Synaesthesia – experienced by the writer Vladimir Nabokov, who reported seeing sounds and hearing colours. People with synaesthesia are not difficult to spot as they would wear earplugs at the Chelsea Flower Show and sunglasses at an AC/DC concert.

3. The Habituation Effect

This refers to the reduction in the strength of a response with repetition. For example, drivers 'habituate' to driving fast on a motorway and so may fail to slow down for exits. For this reason horizontal lines are placed across the road at exits.

Habituation can also be used to simulate levitation in an unsuspecting volunteer. Clearly real levitation is impossible, but it is good fun to bluff. Just ask volunteers to sit on the floor blindfolded while you press down on their shoulders for five minutes. Their brain will habituate to the pressure so when you release your hands they are convinced of a change in an opposite direction, namely a sensation of floating to the ceiling. Insist that this feat is a perfect demonstration of the great usefulness of psychology.

4. Unconscious Cognitive Processes

Psychologists have now shown that the 'unconscious' is not only the preserve of psychoanalysis. The unconscious is rife in studies of perception and attention too. **John Bargh** (pronounced 'Barge' as in boat) from Yale University is the key name to quote. He found that people's behaviour can be affected by words that are presented for a fraction of a second and then masked. Subliminal messages of this sort can have an effect on people's feelings of thirst or hunger, how much they consume, and their choice of product. These highly controlled studies have provided unsettling support for the ideas from the 1970s that 'flash-frames' in television, film and advertising can subtly influence people's behaviour. This can be the only plausible explanation for the popularity of the Bay City Rollers.

Learning

For the sake of argument (and psychologists like a good barney) there are four different kinds of learning. They are:

1. Classical Conditioning (Making links between different experiences, or, more memorably, dribbling to a doorbell.)

Everyone knows about Pavlov and his salivating spaniel, so a cursory comment about him won't pass you off as a psychologist. But if you can pick up the finer details of this surreal experiment, you are in expert territory – even top-grade graduates stumble over this one. First Pavlov rang a bell while the dog was salivating when it saw and smelt some food placed under its nose. Then, the dog salivated to the bell with no food around. It linked (or 'associated' – longer words are always better) the bell and the food in its mind. Now you can easily repeat the study at home if you feel that there aren't already enough slavering dogs in your vicinity.

Though this experiment is easy to remember, the intelligent-sounding terms are designed to confuse, so using them is well worth the bluffing potential they confer. The effect is called 'classical conditioning', or 'associative learning'. (Take your pick.) It works best when the 'conditioned stimulus' or CS (the bell in this case) reliably occurs at the same time as the 'unconditioned stimulus' or UCS (the food). The UCS is defined as an 'innate stimulus' that is by its very nature either pleasurable (e.g., food, sex, comfort, sit-coms with Felicity Kendall) or aversive (e.g., pain, discomfort, Michael Jackson).

At first the CS has no effect on behaviour at all (what is deemed 'neutral' in psycho-speak), but with learning it produces the same effects as the UCS. Thanks to this effect, humans learn to salivate when they see shiny bright chocolate wrappers and learn to walk faster when they see a man on the street with a clipboard.

The most quoted example of conditioning in humans is the study of 'Little Albert' by **John Watson** in 1920 who conditioned a small boy to fear rats by combining the sight of a rat with a loud startling noise. Thankfully such ethically dubious studies are now consigned to history, but they provide regular fascination for generations of psychology undergraduates.

2. **Operant Conditioning** (Using the carrot and the stick, or if you prefer, the whip and the biscuit.)

It may seem like common sense to state that people will do more of something if it leads to a reward ('positive reinforcement') or if it helps them escape punishment ('negative reinforcement') and less of something when it leads to punishment or a lack of a reward ('extinction'). But why call it common sense when you can give it a big name and spend your life testing it on baffled rodents. The classic experiments where rats press a lever to get a food pellet take place in a Skinner Box. It's OK, they don't shave and peel the poor squeakers. The word Skinner comes from the radical behaviourist mentioned earlier who was the greatest champion of operant conditioning.

Skinner believed that the behaviour of animals and humans could be controlled by creating the correct environment, and used his idea as the basis of his vision of a perfect, utopian society. A bit like Sweden but with less herrings and no pine furniture. It is important to know that feelings about B. F. Skinner run deep among psychologists. They see him either as an obsessive, arrogant control freak who brought up his daughter in a box (fortunately a fiction though photos reveal that he did invent a cot for her with a built-in thermostat) or they see him as a misunderstood visionary scientist whose work explains all human behaviour (fortunately also a fiction). You could be radical too and adopt an opinion somewhere in between these two opinions.

American behaviourist **Edward Lee Thorndike** (1874-1949) proposed that behaviour changes through a very gradual process of 'trial-and-error' learning. Or even longer if it involves working out how to use a remote control for digital TV. The popular stereotype of the research psychologist who administers electric shocks to hapless victims during aversion therapy is thankfully rare. Punishment is not only patently unpleasant but also rarely helpful for the basic reason that, while a reward tells people what to do, punishment only tells them what not to do. Clearly, the criminal justice system has yet to fully catch on to this principle.

3. Vicarious Conditioning (Learning from observing others, or being a fashion victim.)

Luckily, people not only learn from their own personal experiences, but also by observing other people. This is called 'observational learning' or 'vicarious conditioning'. (To use both in the same sentence can confound most effectively.) It is particularly strong in children and adolescents who pick up behaviours and attitudes from adult role models, which may include their parents and their teachers but are more likely to be rapper Ice B & Q and the Eee-Zee-Crew.

4. Insight Learning (Learning after one attempt, or being a clever monkey.)

If you think that these simple learning theories all sound a little, well, simple, then you are probably right. As early as the 1920s, the German **Wolfgang Kohler** (1887-1967) demonstrated that chimpanzees could learn through 'insight', working out a problem with no need for intensive trial-and-error learning. As a consequence, most lab rats are now out of a job and looking to retrain as plumbers.

Memory

Faced with a concept to define, like 'memory', psychologists tend to divide it up into smaller bits and then say, 'Well it's made of these bits'. That's all very well as long as you know what the bits are. We can provide you with some simple shorthand so that you can be indistinguishable from a memory specialist.

One way to divide memory is to split it into:

- what you do (memory for actions – **procedural memory**);
- what you know (memory for facts – **semantic memory**), and
- what you've done (memory for experiences – **episodic memory**).

Or you can divide memory into:

- what you know you know (**explicit memory**), and
- what you don't know you know (**implicit memory**).

If these don't make it any easier, it can be divided it into stages. Memory is like filing. When an experience is encoded, you file it away. The file is kept for a while in storage, and when you need the information again you retrieve it. However, this all depends on how good your filing system is.

Memory is normally well organised by a good 'mental secretary'. When the mental secretary is out to lunch (or is tired, stressed, or in a rush), new memories become disorganised or 'fragmented'. They can be as difficult to find as mislaid car keys, or they can pop up when you don't want them to (like pyjamas under your pillow when you're on a romantic date).

Psychologists have found that after major events, people's memory is often disorganised in this way and part of dealing with it is to use the mental secretary to order the memories so that they make sense. This of course relies on the fact that the mental secretary is contactable and not booking an online holiday to Tenerife whilst plugged into her iPod.

The study of memory is one of those areas in psychology that has been researched and speculated about ad infinitum. Your best bet is to commit the big names and ideas to memory and forget the rest. You could use a 'mnemonic' – a strategy to improve memory by linking words with a mental image. For example, **Elizabeth Loftus** demonstrated how memory is not a direct copy of experience; what one learns later on can add to and distort it. This is known as 'reconstructed memory'. You could try to remember this association by imagining the Queen of England (Elizabeth) reconstructing the loft of her house. Or perhaps not.

Never mind if you have difficulty picking up this technique because the facts you learn may be impossible to forget. Psychologists have found little watertight evidence that memories actually fade away with time. The idea that people's experiences, especially traumatic ones, are never truly forgotten was popular with Freud, and all too familiar to people who watched *Dr Who* as a child.

Emotion

If you want a straight answer to what emotion is, you are probably better off asking a playwright rather than a psychologist. The official answer in psychology is, 'I don't really know', but for your information the consensus is that an emotion is made up from at least five different features. For instance, for being 'enthusiastic' we might have:

a) physiology (e.g., heart racing with anticipation);
b) expression (e.g., eyes wide with surprise);
c) behaviour (e.g., shouting out 'I can't wait');
d) cognition (e.g., perceiving a great gain in knowledge),
e) experience (e.g., being aware of all the above).

You may feel that you still don't know what an emotion is but at least you can provide the answer a psychologist would happily provide.

The best way to impress anyone with your knowledge of emotion is to point out that the first scientific study of human emotion was carried out by none other than **Charles Darwin** in *The Expression of the Emotions in Man and Animals* in 1872. This book is far superior to anything produced in the subsequent 130 years and contains reams of text on gestures and facial expressions, with impressive pictures of posing Victorian gentlemen and over-excited Alsatians.

The American psychologist, **Paul Ekman** has worked hard to prove that there are some innate emotions that are the same in all humans around the world and some animals (though presumably not cats, who only know 'smug'). These emotions are fear, anger, disgust, surprise, and happiness. They are known as **basic emotions** and each is indicated by a particular facial expression and activity in a particular part of the brain; but if you experience all of them during one night out then things are unlikely to be straightforward. Just in case you were thinking that psychologists had ruined all the mystery of human emotion, there is a whole range of complex emotions like guilt, pride, nostalgia, and the inner glow after a day of DIY, that defy being explained this way.

Psychologists enjoy doing studies on happiness, laughter and smiling, probably so they can work out how to get more of them. And why not. People who laugh more are rated as being more likeable and attractive. They also have lower levels of stress, healthier immune systems and a reduced experience of pain. But as you will have witnessed during the rush hour, laughter does not come that easily. While children laugh about 400 times per day, adults manage a paltry 18. This may be because the need for play is innate and emerges in childhood as a way of learning social rules and creating bonds. It is found in mammals and birds: chimps and even rats emit a form of laughter during play, although to the casual observer a rat's 'laugh' sounds suspiciously like a squeak.

It is all very well knowing these things but you may ask whether psychology can actually help people to feel happier. Luckily, it seems that laughter and smiling are contagious: there are genuine reports of epidemics of laughter spreading through entire villages in Africa. To measure the contagious effect of smiling, one psychologist even went to the effort of smiling at hundreds of complete strangers in a shopping mall to see how many smiled back – a massive 40%. So recommend your audience to start smiling and (nearly half) the world will smile too.

Psychologists say normal everyday emotions help people communicate and empathise with others. But when emotions are very strong, they hijack the control centres of the brain (in the frontal lobes) and disrupt normal thinking. So it's fine to be a bit anxious when bluffing in psychology; just don't panic.

34

ntelligence

t is worth picking up the finer points of research on ntelligence. Not only does it make you look clever, ut it might even help you become cleverer, if you elieve what some of the theories have to say.

. The Beginnings

Iumans have felt the need to demonstrate their uperiority to one another ever since some of them ould rub two sticks together and others just kept iissing. The field of Intelligence Testing legitimised his petty form of social comparison. It began with ood intentions. At the turn of the 20th century, a rench Psychologist named **Alfred Binet** (the 't' is lent as in 'bidet') developed the first tests to identify hildren who were behind in their abilities and would enefit from specialised teaching. But the tests were oon used for slightly less worthy purposes. In the Jnited States, **Goddard** adapted them (the Stanford-iinet tests) to screen all new recruits to the U.S. rmy. Unfortunately they have never been used to creen U.S. presidents.

One of the first psychologists to try to explain ntelligence was **Charles Spearman**. He proposed hat intelligence was a 'mental energy' that was eflected in people's reaction times – the time to work ut which of two lines is longer provided an indication f intelligence. Of course, if this was true then clever eople would never get into the wrong queue at the upermarket.

. The Nature-versus-Nurture Debate

Iany people began to claim that intelligence was ntirely a product of genetics. **Frances Galton** coined

the phrase 'nature versus nurture' and set out t
prove that the balance was definitely tilted toward
the former. **Cyril Burt** presented data for the stron
effects of genes on intelligence that was literally to
good to be true. It appears that he had fabricated hi
results – a dangerous example of a man who bluffe
too far. In the nature-vs-nurture debate the curren
consensus is reliably straight down the middle: "Bot
are important." You might want to embellish this b
going on to say that of course this "all depends on hov
you measure intelligence and what sample you use"
For example, measuring emotional intelligence i
regimental sergeant majors could really skew you
findings.

3. What Is IQ?

To bluff in Intelligence Testing successfully, you nee
only take on board a few elementary facts about I
(Intelligence Quotient) so that you can beat psycholo
gists at their own game.

The average IQ of any population is 100, and 99
of people score between 65 and 135. It is important t
realise that if a person scores much outside thi
range, IQ becomes almost impossible to measure fo
the simple reason that there are too few very cleve
people around on whom to properly perfect ver
clever versions of the tests. So if someone tells yo
that their IQ is 182 then they are intelligent enoug
to know better. The good news to promulgate is tha
one might catch up anyway. Performance on IQ test
is known to improve through practice, so advocat
keeping up the effort.

A big question asked by some psychologists, an
conveniently ignored by others, is whether IQ test
are any use at all. Psychologists have found that IQ
only mildly related to success in the real world (e.g

status, occupation, earnings), and above a certain value it has no validity whatsoever. Factors such as family background and practical skills are more important. Nobel prize winners cannot be distinguished from their less successful peers on the basis of their IQ scores. People are quite encouraged by the fact that they may still be a genius even if their IQ is not shooting through the roof.

4. There Is More Than One Way to Be Intelligent

During the last century, psychologists argued over whether intelligence could be divided up into smaller parts, or factors, and if so, how many – i.e., how many slices can divide up a cake. The answer ranged from a stingy two (Spearman), through seven (Thurstone) to a generous 120 (Guilford). Needless to say the psychologists testing Guilford's theory had their work cut out, and all 120 factors have never been found. Thurstone's factors are most familiar: verbal comprehension, fluency, arithmetic, spatial skills, memory, perceptual speed and reasoning.

It may be easier to remember American psychologist **Raymond Cattell**'s two kinds of intelligence: 'fluid' and 'crystallised'. You may occasionally entertain grave doubts about contestants on TV quiz shows who know obscure trivia but look as if they couldn't find their way out of the studio. According to Cattell, they may be high on 'crystallised intelligence' (in essence, facts and figures they have crammed) but could well be in the bottom stream when it comes 'fluid intelligence' (novel ways of thinking – more useful in the real world). While crystallised intelligence remains the same over a lifetime, fluid intelligence starts to decline from around 40 years of age. Clearly the younger you learn to bluff the better.

Later on in the 20th century, psychologists began to develop even more interesting views of intelligence. **Howard Gardner** proposed a form of intelligence for nearly every area of expertise – multiple intelligences. His theory is a great confidence-builder. For example, a premiership footballer may have a high Kinesthetic Intelligence (physical skills) despite a low Linguistic Intelligence (being monosyllabic). Conversely, a distinguished professor who may have a high Logico-mathematical Intelligence may be a dunce in Interpersonal Intelligence (missing other people's signs of boredom). Why not add to this theory by researching your own particular form of intelligence: for example, Cryptic Intelligence – the ability to complete *The Times* crossword in less than three weeks.

In the 1980s, **Robert Sternberg** came up with three 'sub' theories for the price of one. Although sounding complicated, the key ideas were so simple it was embarrassing that no-one had thought of them before. The 'contextual subtheory' pointed out that what may seem intelligent behaviour in one environment may be completely irrelevant in another. For example, navigating by the stars is very useful in the Red Sea, but useless on the London Underground. Conversely, honing the skills to get top score on Grand Turismo III is unlikely to equip a teenager for a life in the outback of Australia. The 'componential subtheory' suggested that intelligence can be understood by splitting it into stages or components. The 'experiential subtheory' basically states that in a test people use more practised knowledge and less novel insight. The latter is thought to be the better measure of the essence of intelligence, leading to the interesting effect (which you simply must try to slip into a conversation) that the more you practise doing intelligence tests, the less they actually measure your real intelligence.

Another area you may have encountered is Emotional Intelligence, the view that people differ in their ability to manage their own emotions and those of others. Take care because use of the term 'Emotional Intelligence' is likely to mark you out as a reader of non-fiction rather than an expert in psychology. On no account use the term 'EQ' (Emotional Quotient) in the same breath as IQ, or your cover will be blown. Instead, state confidently that emotional intelligence is too value laden (psychology is not without its political stance), and anyway it is so closely correlated with most other measures of intelligence as to be virtually meaningless (the greatest insult in psychology, which after all has the lofty goal of trying to see the meaning in everything).

5. Things Can Only Get Better

A good bluffing point in the study of intelligence is 'The Flynn Effect'. Despite how it may appear from the quality of day-time television, people in the Western world have been getting more intelligent every decade since the 1930s, and are continuing to do so. Explanations vary from improved education and better nutrition to more practice assembling flat-packed furniture.

Personality

You will now be familiar with psychologists' flare at defining everyday things and dividing them into different bits, each with an elaborate new name. Psychologists seem to take as much interest in defining something in the first place as they do studying it. Personality is no exception. Psychologists manage to agree that personality is something that is a quality of a person, that it leads a person to be consistent in his or her behaviour in different situations, and that each person differs in whatever it is. Any famous psychologist worth their salt seems to have had their hand in a theory of personality: Sigmund Freud, Carl Jung, B. F. Skinner and Carl Rogers are a few examples. As a would-be expert in the psychology of personality, you need to know the basic essentials of what has been covered over the centuries.

1. Personality Types: Greek Body Juices

Your starting point for pontificating about personality is Ancient Greece (in such a recent discipline like psychology it always impresses to go back more than a century, and citing an ancient civilisation is a trump card). Back then, **Galen** (A.D. 130-200) suggested that personality is made up from the balance of four types of bodily fluids. While modern-day psychologists are clearly sceptical about the fluid idea, the names of these four types of fluids remain. All you need in order to commit these to memory for instant use is a nodding acquaintance with *Winnie-the-Pooh*, since each personality type matches a character from the book. First is blood (**sanguine** – confident and cheerful – Christopher Robin); second is phlegm (**phlegmatic** – placid and unphased – Owl); third is black bile (**melancholic** – anxious and depressed – Eeyore), and last of all is yellow bile (**choleric** – lively and unpredictable – Tigger). Bluffing psychology really is child's play.

2. Personality Traits: Two-dimensional characters

It is generally agreed that by the 1960s it was time for a slightly more advanced way of dividing up personality than oozing visceral liquids. Though you may choose to wonder. The British psychologist, **H. J Eysenck** proposed just two personality traits: 'Neuroticism' and 'Introversion-Extroversion'. Each person gets a score on both traits, so a person could be represented by a single point on a piece of graph paper. What a nice personal touch.

Meanwhile, on the other side of the Atlantic, Raymond Cattell (who, like Eysenck, dabbled in both personality and intelligence) was understandably convinced that people were a bit more complex than Eysenck had thought, and embarked on an ambitious project to establish 16 personality factors – 'the 16PF'. He used the Lexical Method, which involves listing and classifying all the personality words in the English language (e.g., grumpy, sneezy, bashful, dopey...). Sadly, no-one else managed to find all 16 of his factors, so for a while psychologists settled for Eysenck's idea that people's personalities were as simple as a single point on a square.

You will be pleased to hear that there is a modern-day compromise to this dilemma – the 'middle-way' again (psychologists should start a new political party). Five personality traits are recognised:

- Openness to experience
- Conscientiousness
- Extroversion
- Agreeableness
- Neuroticism

(O.C.E.A.N.). Acronyms are widespread in psychology and give the impression of breezy familiarity with the subject, so always drop a few.

Interestingly, a study has shown that people in the U.S. and Italy rate politicians on only two personality traits rather than five, which could explain a great deal. If you are convinced that your pet has a personality,

41

then you are probably right. The same personality traits are reflected in the behaviour of dogs and horses. The fact that there is less data on cats may be because they felt that the tests were beneath them.

3. Psychometric Tests: Being honest about oneself

The simplest way to assess personality is to ask people questions about themselves. Always refer to this as Psychometric Testing because it has a wonderful air of scientific rigour, as though it could be anywhere near as exact as measuring someone's height, weight or cholesterol level.

You may have had the unfortunate experience of a psychometric test when applying for a job. "Do you generally get on with other people?" is a fine example of an item on a personality questionnaire. Your instincts may be telling you that such a transparent method will be clearly flawed. You are unlikely to answer this question with the response: "No, for I fear they are Satan!", and far more likely to say "Yes" even if it is, God forbid, a lie. But, as a seasoned bluffer in psychology, you must never call this lying. It is far more grand: "The Social Desirability Effect" – the tendency for people to ignore their weaknesses and portray themselves in a positive light.

There is an important lesson for bluffing here. Whenever there is an obvious flaw in your argument that is apparent to everyone around you, don't be phased. You must say with great self-assurance that this is not a flaw at all but the operation of another important psychological process of which you were already fully aware. In fact you have been researching it. Here is when your powers of imagination come into play. Make up a phrase to label it, which will always begin with 'The' and end with 'Effect'. The middle is

42

up to you, and the more obscure and ponderous the better. "The Indirect McCollough Effect" is a real example and "The Coaxial Reverse Bunion Effect" isn't. But no-one will know the difference.

4. Projective Tests: Sussing out your subject

One of the ways that psychologists can assess personality without being caught out by people's fibbing is to assess their personalities more sneekily. You will already be acquainted with the famous inkblot test. Note for future reference that it was devised by a Swiss psychiatrist in the 1940s. You should also refer to it by his name, the Rorschach Test (pronounce the 'shack' part with a healthy curdle of spittle to emphasise your cosmopolitan credentials). The Rorschach is an example of a 'projective test'. It encourages people to reveal elements of their personality in how they describe what they see. The genuine rules of how to interpret these blobs are disproportionately complicated and best left well alone. But your audience will be convinced that you know something they don't if you dwell thoughtfully on their answer, mutter something about 'the emphasis on the depth of form' and announce your assessment with poise: "You are a moderately shy person who is kind-hearted and wants to be better understood by other people." Most people will find it difficult to disagree with this perspicacious analysis of their inner psyche, and will assume you have magical powers.

5. Objective Tests: The ultimate goal

Of course projective tests are in practice even more unreliable than the self-report methods. Psychologists have tried in earnest (and they are often very earnest) to find the real scientific method of assessing personality – the 'objective test'. There has been very little progress at all, but some interesting titbits have come up that you would do well to slip into any dinner party conversation. For example, studies show that extroverts spend more time talking to people and neurotic people sit much further away when being interviewed. Presumably this means that neurotic extroverts have booming voices.

A more head-turning finding is that introverts are also more easily aroused. The evidence on which this conclusion is based is rather disappointing: introverts produce more saliva when they taste a drop of lemon juice. No-one has yet tested this theory in people's reactions to pictures of Halle Berry.

Language

Most of the psychology of language, or psycholinguistics, is fiendishly complicated and tedious, and therefore best left unexplored. You need know only one major name: **Noam Chomsky**. Before his rather more stimulating career in international affairs he developed a theory of language. He came up with the idea of Universal Grammar. Many people, especially if they are British, don't understand what foreign language speakers are saying. But Chomsky argued that every language of the world shares the same fundamental grammar. It is an innate structure, and the same across different cultures. However, this theory may seem rather academic when you are trying to get directions to the nearest tourist information office in downtown Mombassa.

It is worth buffing up on another contentious topic in the psychology of language called the 'linguistic-relativity hypothesis'. It states that language affects the way that people perceive the world. The most often cited evidence for this view is that Greenland Inuits have approximately 400 words for snow. This is complete hokum that has become exaggerated over the years. The real answer is nearer a dozen. You could capitalise on this by pointing out that twelve is not much more than in English (e.g., blizzard, hail, flurry, sleet, slush, etc.).

The last part of the psychology of language worth knowing, because of its constant fascination, is talking to animals. Of course, talking to them is easy. It is getting them to talk back that is the hard part.

Though the efforts of David Attenborough may be hard to emulate, never mind Dr Doolittle, several animals have been taught to communicate using 'language'. This star line-up includes Sarah the chimp, Koko the gorilla, Alex the parrot and Kanzi the pygmy chimpanzee. But don't begin a book club with your neighbourhood canine friends just yet. The most competent level an animal has achieved so far is that of a 2-year-old child and this required intensive training by devoted researchers. It may be easier for you to learn how to woof.

SOCIAL PSYCHOLOGY

The only bit that people are interested in here, is body language. It is a common fact that psychologists know everything there is to know about body language. It is a lesser known fact that actually they don't, unless they are experts on 'non-verbal behaviour' (never call it 'body language' or your cover will be blown). Displaying a modicum of knowledge about non-verbal behaviour will come in handy during your double life as a psychologist and there are really only three things you need to know:

1. How to Appear Dominant

According to researchers on body language people appear more dominant when they look taller, stand with their hands on their hips, interrupt people, face towards the people they talk to, stare into their eyes as they talk to them (but not when listening to them), adopt an expression of anger, smile with closed lips and speak in basso profundo tones. You might feel that such behaviour could indeed make a person appear dominant, but precious few would hang around to see it.

2. How to Detect Whether Someone Is Lying

While most people believe that shifty eyes and fidgety hands are sure signs of lying, these are chronically misleading. Psychologists feel that lying is better regarded as a struggle between unconscious 'leakage' of a person's feelings and conscious attempts to mask this leakage. The best indications of lying are 'micro-momentary expressions' – the leakage of feelings that last a fraction of a second. Apparently, Bill Clinton's face was riddled with these expressions during his classic Monica Lewinsky denials.

3. How to Know if Someone Is Attracted to You

The gestures that psychologists have identified as indicating attraction are: prolonged eye contact, fluttering of eyelids, flicking of hair, tilting the head, showing the neck, caressing objects, pouting, and smiling. These signs have an added function. If prospective partners miss these gestures then you know to avoid them because they are unlikely to be gifted with great sensitivity.

BRAIN AND BEHAVIOUR

A good reason not to learn about the brain is that if you want to be indistinguishable from a psychologist then you only need to know as much about it as the average psychologist, which is very little. Typically, a psychologist will argue that what the brain does and how it does it are more important than which parts of the brain are involved. Of course, there are specialists within psychology who do study the brain, but they tend to be a dubious collection of characters who mainly enjoy zapping people with radiation and passing huge magnetic waves through their skulls. This gives them an exciting sense of power, regardless of whether they find any sensible results.

DEVELOPMENTAL PSYCHOLOGY

This is the study of the development of cognition and behaviour from birth to adulthood. It is very handy to know. Not only can you pass yourself off in yet another field of psychology, but also it helps you to see screaming toddlers in a whole new light – that of the developmental psychologist's glaring lamp as he or she scrutinises their every move.

The early psychologist William James believed that infants understood very little and that the world of an infant was a 'buzzing blooming confusion'. This was a reasonable way to get out of trying to study them at all. Eventually, in the 1950s, the French psychologist **Jean Piaget** took the bold step of actually trying to find out what children could understand. He managed to develop an entire theory of development based on observing his own children. One reason his ideas had an enduring appeal to other psychologists may be because he saw his children as just like them: little scientists who test out their theories in the world, bring in new information (assimilation), and update their ideas (accommodation) when they find out something new. You will have noted by now that five-syllable words ending in '-ation' can act as nuggets of knowledge in the cunning bluffer's vocabulary (e.g., 'assimilation', 'accommodation', 'association', 'habituation'). If at a loss for an imposing word to use in conversation, just mutter unintelligibly and end it with '-ation' or '-ition' (e.g., "Of course, this is clearly the well-known effect of hhrrrmmfffferr…ation").

It is important for you to state that Piaget's ideas, however influential, were based only on his own children's behaviour. This will mark you out as a true scientist. Whether Piaget actually checked if the tiny tearaways who lived over the road also fitted his model is not known. You will also want to talk of **object permanence** – the understanding that objects continue to exist when they are out of view. Piaget believed that this ability developed at around 12 months old, although many adults have this difficulty when it involves dirty dishes or ironing.

Piaget hogged the limelight for developmental psychology for over 30 years until psychologists decided to try testing his theories in detail. They capitalised on the fact known by any parent that babies get bored easily – they 'habituate' to things that are familiar with and look longer at things that are unexpected. Interestingly the amount a baby habituates to a new object at 7 months predicts its IQ at 5 years old. Using habituation, the American child psychologist, **Renée Baillargeon** revealed babies to be rather cleverer than Piaget had given them credit for. Baillargeon created a whole series of studies involving cuddly toys, moving screens and secret trapdoors more akin to a child's magic show than a psychology laboratory. The clever tots in these experiments knew that objects existed when out of sight at three months, not one year as Piaget had thought, and they could even do elementary problem-solving at six months. So, never underestimate the mind of a baby. They know much more than they let on.

If your aim in bluffing psychology is to get an easy life, then maybe you should emulate another child psychologist, **Andy Meltzoff**. He made his first scientific breakthrough by pulling silly faces at newborn babies. He found that they could imitate simple facial gestures, such as an 'o' shaped mouth. He then progressed to clowning around trying to throw a hoop over a hook and missing every time. He found that 18-month-old babies got it right first time – they imitated his intention, not his behaviour. His final innovation was to wait for a day or so. He found that infants could copy his intentions 24 hours later.

A key idea in developmental psychology is **Theory of Mind**. This is the awareness that other people have a different perception of the world from one's own and it develops around three years of age. The skill helps people to communicate effectively and appreciate humour, but more importantly it enables humans to fib, prevaricate and of course, bluff.

CLINICAL PSYCHOLOGY

A popular stereotype of a psychologist is the bearded male therapist whose patient lies supine on a couch talking in intimate detail about his mother. The modern therapist is more likely to be a non-bearded woman who sits at a desk with her patients on hard plastic chairs planning a helpful schedule of next week's daily activities. The couch is either missing or used to watch daytime television.

Contrary to received wisdom, you do not need to know the Ancient Greek names of obscure phobias because English is now accepted. For example, the intriguing 'alektorophobia' becomes the more mundane, 'chicken phobia', and the somewhat intimidating 'Hippopotomonstrosesquippedaliphobia' becomes 'long word phobia'.

Strictly speaking, clinical psychology refers to the use of psychological theories and methods in clinical settings, i.e., hospital basements. However, you should be aware that knowledge of these complicated ideas is really only necessary as a last resort. For a start, many patients will get better even if the clinical psychologist does absolutely nothing. There are several reasons for this:

1. **Natural Remission** – Some just will get better.

2. **The Placebo Effect** – As soon as patients walk through the door of a psychologist's office their expectation of a successful treatment (however dubious that may be) actually leads them to improve.

3. **The Confession-box Effect** – People's symptoms can improve just by talking or writing them down, even if there is no response.

4. **Normalisation** – Being able to tell someone one's innermost thoughts without them running for the door is probably therapeutic in itself. It turns out that most of the things people are worried about, like having disturbing thoughts, scary dreams, impulses to shout rude words in church, are statistically 'normal'. Just being told this is a relief in itself.

A common view is that psychological therapies are all pretty much the same. While this may have some truth in practice, principled bluffers should announce their differences with self-possessed gusto. You can easily get away with knowing something about just four different therapies:

Client-Centred Therapy (or 'nodding' therapy)

This is a school of thought that provides an excuse to do very little as a therapist. According to its founder, **Carl Rogers**, the therapist merely needs to provide what he termed Unconditional Positive Regard. In essence this means one should be nice and empathic towards a patient whatever they say or do. And not require them to do anything.

When the therapist realises that her life is passing her by while she is grinning and nodding to comments about the weather (or not), she may become desperate to encourage some action on the part of the patient, which is where the next form of therapy fits in.

Behaviour Therapy (or 'nudging' therapy)

Behaviour therapy certainly makes more demands. It proposes **Graded Exposure** as a form of treatment. Despite the name, Graded Exposure does not involve stripping naked and dying slowly on a cold mountain. It means gradually facing one's fears a step at a time. Rome wasn't built in a day after all.

An alternative technique in Behaviour Therapy with an equally appealing name is **Flooding** – confronting one's worst fear all at once (such as throwing a spider phobic into a vat full of tarantulas). Unsurprisingly, strict versions of this technique faded out of use about the same time as public flogging. Cognitive Therapy (q.v.) replaced these terms with the more scientific-sounding term, Behavioural Experiments, in which a patient's predictions of what may happen in a situation (for example, "I will spontaneously combust on reading Welsh poetry") are tested against the reality ("I didn't").

Cognitive Therapy (or 'noodling' therapy, as in 'use your noodle')

Cognitive Therapy (or Cognitive Behavioural Therapy o CBT) is the most scientifically supported form o psychological therapy and it appears easy to pick up - making it easy to bluff. Unfortunately this means that other people are already bluffing in it too. So the strategy is to outbluff the bluffers.

Amateurs think that CBT is all about positive thinking; in fact, CBT is more to do with thinking about thinking – 'metacognition' is the buzzword. This simply means it is OK to have a thought like "I am useless" – this is normal, especially for psychologists. But if you think that this thought must be true just because you've thought it, then you've got problems.

Aaron T. (for 'Tim') Beck created cognitive therapy in the 1960s. According to Beck the rock on which cognitive therapy is founded is called 'collaborative empiricism'. Don't be phased. This is a posh phrase for the therapist and patient working together to test the patient's beliefs. As it is Professor Beck's avowed intention to know everyone in the world who practises CBT, it should be possible to make people believe you know him. Casually refer to your last chat with 'Tim about "the activation of latent dysfunctional assumptions" and you will be accepted as one of the crew.

A useful principle also used in cognitive therapy is The Vicious Cycle – not a Penny Farthing with spiky wheels but a 'heuristic' that shows that the way people try to cope with their problems can make the problem worse, or even more simply, the solution becomes the problem. Solution-focused therapy is based on this principle too. For example, a vicious cycle of binge-eating is:

I get upset → I eat lots → I get fat → I get upset – I eat lots, etc.

Once the penny drops that there is a vicious cycle, people can often learn to behave differently and extract themselves from this circular trap. However, whether or not vicious cycles help in therapy, they have the added bonus of helping you appreciate the beautiful yet pointless circularity of human behaviour everywhere. Life really is a merry-go-round.

Systemic/Family Therapy ('canoodling' therapy)

This therapy proposes that a person's symptoms must be understood in the context of their past and present relationships. Whole families are invited to air their dirty laundry in front of a team of psychologists, all but one of whom escape behind a one-way mirror. It begins with the creation of a **Dendrogram** (psychologists' scientific-sounding word for a family tree) which not only includes the complete family but also 'significant others', plus symbols to represent births, deaths, marriages, divorces, sex, living arrangements, noisy neighbours and shoe sizes.

If a budding psychologist can complete this elaborate diagram by the end of the therapy session then he or she would deserve to be regarded as an expert regardless of what happens to the patients.

And the Rest...

You may feel that there is a slight gap in this section: disorders of the mind have barely been mentioned. There is good reason for this. First, describing the distressing symptoms of mental illness is intrinsically unamusing, as we are sure you will agree. Second, while psychiatrists have inherited the tendency within medicine to organise and label everything, and have therefore carried out the arduous task of classifying over 350 mental disorders (the categorical approach) psychologists generally feel this is excessively keen Their research suggests that this may not be worth all the effort because the key features of a disorder are very similar (the 'trans-diagnostic' approach). Some would even say they are non-existent and are created by society (the 'social-constructivist' approach).

So your best bet is to claim that: "The classification of different psychological disorders is largely redundant when it comes to providing treatment." Making this claim is likely to win over the more progressive psychologists to your side, and infuriate most psychiatrists in the process, which is a sweet sight to behold. They will believe that you could not possibly make such a smug statement without being a genuine radical psychologist.

POSITIVE PSYCHOLOGY AND POSITIVE PSYCHOTHERAPY

While many psychologists are obsessed with people's suffering and playing tricks on people's minds, some have used their skills to try to increase the tonnage of happiness in the world. The well-known American psychologist, **Marty Seligman**, coined a term for this pursuit – **Positive Psychology**. (Obviously one is meant to assume that the rest of psychology is Negative or Neutral Psychology.) Becoming acquainted with Positive Psychology can be a great boon. As a would be expert in this area, you can claim to be finding out the secret of achieving happiness whilst having more fun than the average psychologist.

If you thought that happiness is all about hedonistic pursuits like gambling and driving fast cars then think again. According to Seligman, there are three elements: The Meaningful Life, The Engaged Life and the Happy Life. 'The Good Life' is not mentioned even though the opportunity to breed pigs with Felicity Kendall would clearly bring lifelong fulfilment to anyone.

The Meaningful Life is said to be part of something bigger than yourself, such as a family, a religion, or a tiddlywinks club. The Engaged Life is being involved in the flow' of what you are doing, like playing the violin or a very involving game of Twister. The key name to bluff with in this area is the psychologist who wrote the best-selling book, *Flow: The Psychology of Optimal Experience*, Mihaly Csikszentmihalyi. If you can pronounce his name then you will be a step ahead of most of his contemporaries (here's the trick – Cheeks-sent-me-high'). The Happy Life involves laughter, feeling good and having fun. So no surprises there then.

Positive Psychotherapy is about how to improve people's happiness and well-being in the long term. Most of the exercises can be boiled down to regularly being nice to yourself and other people, but on no account let on that it is quite that simple. The unexpected thing is not the fact that this works, but how little people do it in the course of their everyday lives, and the impact it can have. In one study, psychologists analysed a short piece of text that 140 nuns had written to sum up their attitudes towards joining a convent. Only a third of the nuns used positive words in their plans. When they were followed up 50 years later, over 90% of the positive-word group were still alive, but 50% of the nuns who had not used positive words had perished. So, getting happy is easy and it might help you live longer. The difficult bit, as the study with the nuns illustrates, is changing one's habits'.

PARAPSYCHOLOGY

Parapsychology refers to the scientific study of what are claimed to be supernatural phenomena. Most psychologists view the work of psychics, astrologists, seers and spoon-benders as the rest of us view time share salesmen. Here are four findings that you can use to enhance your status as an expert:

1. People tend to notice, remember and believe what fits in with their expectations. This can reach an extreme in otherwise 'normal' people: studies show that up to 80% of grieving relatives actually halluci nate their deceased loved one during the months after the death (yes, hallucinations are normal). So, the bereaved are ripe for tricks of perception and unwill ing to believe they are being duped.

2. **Cold reading** involves making a prediction that sounds unlikely but is in fact very common. For exam ple, if asked to think of one shape inside another shape, people invariably think of a circle inside a triangle or vice versa. About 40% of people have a scar on one knee, and "You are experiencing financial difficulties at the moment" is true of almost everyone even a multi-millionaire.

3. **Sensory leakage** is a great indicator. Psychics as well as psychologists are aware that people communi cate via body language and other subtle cues that give things away. For example, at the beginning of the century a German horse called 'Clever Hans' was thought to be able to perform arithmetic by tapping out the answer with his hoof in the presence of his owner. The skill was attributed to telepathy until a psychologist discovered that the horse was respond ing to subtle gestures that the owner was emitting.

4. An **outside force**. Psychics can claim that they tap into a 'force' that is outside their own control. This not only prevents them looking too big-headed in claiming their own enormous powers, but it can be used to explain when things go wrong. The psychic can claim that there is a poor 'connection' with the force today, rather like the excuses rail companies give for a late train.

BIG QUESTIONS IN PSYCHOLOGY

Your ability to bluff in psychology is now likely to have come on a treat. However, you may need some big guns to bring out when the stakes get high. For this you need a few answers to Big Questions – the kind that appear unknowable and inspire the work of philosophers, novelists, playwrights and television illusionists alike. Here are a few belters:

Do We Have Free Will?

Day-long discussions on this topic are normally the preserve of philosophers, but in the quest for evidence psychologists will happily poach on any preserve. A study designed by **Benjamin Libet** tested people on the exact time they felt 'the urge to move'. The answer (about half a second after the first detectable impulse arose in the brain) seemed to confirm that the unconscious brain was in complete control. You can point out that this sinister claim proved to be poppycock since later studies showed that people deliberately prepare themselves to move (like at the start of a 100-metre sprint), so humans do have free will – it's just a tad sluggish.

What Is Consciousness?

Consciousness is the Holy Grail of psychologists, neuroscientists, biologists, philosophers and physicists, and just as difficult to find. Theories abound, from it being nothing more than an after-effect of the physical processes of the brain through to the idea that it is people's private simulation of the world inside their heads. Of course, the real purpose of consciousness is in providing employment. It is an ever-moving target that can be never fully understood and so it keeps an appreciable minority of the academic community off the streets.

What Is Humour?

1. The Superiority Theory – First proposed by the Greek philosopher Plato (427-348 B.C.), this states that humour involves feeling superior to someone else, such as the person who slips on a banana skin (which interestingly people only ever seem to do in cartoons and comedies and not in real life).

2. Repressed Thought Theory – Freud naturally considered that humour allows a person to express repressed thoughts about sex, marriage, bodily functions and aggression in a socially acceptable way. An example: 'For fifteen years my husband and I were the happiest people in the world. Then we met.'

3. Incongruity Theory – This is the idea that we laugh at things that surprise us because they seem out of place. In other words, they conflict with our expectations. Psychologists have shown that there is a moment of confusion that is then explained by the punchline, which they flatly term the 'incongruity resolution'. For example: Two fish in a tank. One says, 'How do you drive this thing?'

What Is the Power of Religion?

Clearly science cannot test out religious views with evidence because they are based on 'faith' - otherwise known to many psychologists as an 'irrational belief'. But psychologists have looked at the effects of being religious, and found that being religious leads to greater happiness and improved health. So if you have your best interests at heart, we advise you to stop trying to learn psychology and get into God in a big way.

Is There Life after Death?

The near-death experience is another golden egg for psychologists. It sounds like such an appealing experience to be drifting towards a light at the end of a tunnel to meet all your long lost friends and relatives, even if they are a little smelly. The last thing you would want to do is to try to explain this visitation as just 'disturbed brain activity'. But it seems that scientists can trigger very similar experiences by stimulating certain regions of the brain with a magnetic field (TMS – transcranial magnetic stimulation). Of course, some volunteers in these studies might start having visions of death as soon as they see the psychologist wielding a huge magnet round their heads.

Why Can't People Tickle Themselves?

Apparently it is the fact that a tickle is unpredictable that makes it ticklish. Sarah Blakemore, daughter of British neuroscientist Colin Blakemore, spent her early academic career inventing and testing a robotic machine that enabled people to tickle themselves. It worked by adding a delay into the tickle, making it unpredictable, and therefore more ticklish. The participants in the study had themselves in stitches.

THE GLOSSARY (Psychobabble)

Body language – What most people believe psychologists study.

Coaction effect – The finding that people work harder when other people are present compared with when they are alone. It appears that psychologists are to blame for the ubiquitous rise of the open-plan office.

Collective unconscious – Not a sleep-over after a big house party, but term coined by Carl Jung (1875-1961) which reflects the shared experiences humans have had in their evolutionary past, e.g., the sun setting and rising, regular meetings with the wise shaman, running away from grizzly bears.

Counterfactual thinking – Thinking of things that might never occur, like being let off with a caution by a speed camera.

Ergonomics – The study of the efficiency of persons in their natural environment; a field of research that has yet to impact on Directory Enquiries.

Educational Psychology – The testing of one or two kids in the class who are driving the teachers out of their minds.

Forensic Psychology – (Popularly) generating the 'psychological profiles' of hunted criminals (e.g., angry, evasive, worrying affection for axes, etc).

Freudian slip – Accidentally coming out with a word that expresses one's deep unconscious fannies.

Heuristic – Simple, efficient rule-of-thumb that can be used to work through a range of problems. Can come in very handy as long as you can work out what it is.

Homunculus – A little man inside the head who is doing all the clever stuff that hasn't been properly explained by a psychological theory. Telling another psychologist that his theory implies there is a homunculus in the brain is the worst insult and is therefore very common.

Incubation phase – Gap between no conscious effort to work on a problem and the moment of 'illumination'. A great excuse to sit in the pub during the day as a work deadline looms. Just say you are waiting for the moment of illumination, which will hopefully arrive before the moment of dismissal.

Lateral thinking – Thinking sideways, a skill that has evolved for solving unlikely quizzes.

Least Effort, Principle of – The notion that the least effort will be expended by a human or animal that is necessary for survival. This principle wields its power in railway staff across the nation.

Occupational Psychology – The study of goings-on in the workplace (i.e., investigating the strange noises in the store-cupboard at the office party).

Perceptual Control Theory – Theory of the mind (of 1970s vintage) that literally turns contemporary psychology on its head by explaining how people (or animals) control their own environment. Great bluffing parry in any exchange with a psychologist.

Persona – The side of ourselves that we present to other people, i.e., most of it in the case of politicians, actors and supermodels.

Pop-out effect – Finding that certain objects in a scene can be spotted without consciously scanning for them, e.g., Uncle Fred at a swingers' party.

Projection – Seeing your own faults in other people.

Also known as 'The pot calling the kettle black'.

Reaction times – The few thousandths of a second that nerve signals take to pass from the senses through the brain to trigger a response, which means that no-one ever truly experiences the present, only the immediate past. Much of cognitive psychology is based on accurately measuring this, so the best way to upset cognitive psychologists as a volunteer in their experiments is to do every task extremely slowly.

Schemas – Stored representations of events, objects and relationships in the real world. People have schemas for every kind of situation, including dating, buying a coffee, and convincing complete strangers that you are a bona fide psychologist.

Tip-of-the-tongue phenomenon – Forgetting something that one knows one knows.

'Type A' personality – Coined by cardiologist Meyer Friedman in the 1950s. People with this trait are aggressive and impatient and have higher rates of coronary heart disease. It's a point worth remembering when you get flashed by a BMW driver inches behind you on the motorway.

Withdrawal symptoms – Unpleasant physiological and psychological reactions when a) an addicted person is denied the source of addiction; b) a psychologist is prevented from talking about psychology for a few hours.

Working memory – Current memory (coined by the British cognitive psychologist, Alan Baddeley) for the information that people are holding in their minds, e.g., telephone numbers, shopping lists and images of Demi Moore in fatigues.

REVERSE GLOSSARY (or How to Substitute Common Phrases with Psychologisms)

You see what you want to see – "Selective processing"

Having a chat – "Engaging in informal social interaction"

That made me jump – "I have encountered a stimulus that has activated my startle reflex"

Love – "Unconditional positive regard"

How was it for you? – "Describe to me your phenomenological experience"

Big-headed – "Suffering from delusions of grandeur"; "Having narcissistic personality traits"

Hitting a raw nerve – "Schema activation"

Taking it out on someone (or something) else – "Displacement"

Being paranoid – "Making an external personal (non-situational) attribution"

You are a pervert – "You have paraphilic tendencies"

In a muddle – "Conceptual disorganisation"

Taking it personally – "Making an internal dispositional attribution"

Stop worrying – "Suppress your self-focused recurrent catastrophic thinking"

Thinking in black and white – "Dichotomous thinking"

Sour grapes – "Rationalisation"

Having a hug – "Attachment behaviour towards the primary caregiver"; "Returning to a secure base"

THE AUTHOR

Warren Mansell nearly became a hard scientist with his first degree in Natural Sciences at the University of Cambridge, but unexpectedly developed into a soft one and turned to Psychology instead.

After a brief sojourn in the real world (publishing), he escaped to the dreaming spires of Oxford where he attempted the Experimental Method (that is to say he did a PhD, or a D.Phil in the case of Oxford who have to be different). A different training in London as a clinical psychologist followed. At 'The Institute' (or IOP), he was surrounded by erudite psychiatrists who enlightened him about the workings of the brain, which he likens to a small doughnut factory, though rather more grey and squidgy and distinctly lacking in jam.

Author of several papers in psychology that involve real science, and far more than he likes to admit that speculate on untested (or untestable) theories, his life-long ambition is to play tiddlywinks with Felicity Kendall. Having recently moved out of the Oxbridge-London triangle he now spends his working days at the University of Manchester showing people cartoons to put them in a happy mood. It's a hard life.

Further titles in the Bluffer's® Guide series:
www.bluffers.com